GENERAL WITHOUT A GUN

GENERAL
WITHOUT A GUN

The Life of William Booth,
Founder of the Salvation Army,
for Teens

by
CHARLES LUDWIG

ZONDERVAN PUBLISHING HOUSE
GRAND RAPIDS, MICHIGAN

Contents

Illustrations

GENERAL WITHOUT A GUN

General William Booth in 1890 — a popular portrait

Chapter One

In the Beginning

HE SHIFTED HIS FEET NERVOUSLY on the heavily carpeted floor as he waited for the exact moment to arrive. A busy man without a moment to waste in his battles for the Lord, he had worked right up to the last few minutes, doused his face hurriedly in a workingman's bucket, called a cab, and frightened the driver by ordering him to head for Buckingham Palace.

The royal servants who waited to take him into the august presence of King Edward VII saw an old man with a soft, flowing, white beard. His finely shaped head was covered with a thick crown of snowy hair and his long hooked nose reminded them of a prophet with a burning message to proclaim.

As he sat in the great room where only the famous are privileged to enter, he wore the uniform of a general. No armed guards had come with him, nor had there been any demonstration heralding his coming, for he was the general of the Salvation Army and his only weapon was a sword — the Sword of the Spirit.

Since he had built up one of the largest spiritual forces in the world, his name was known everywhere. He had met and chatted with many of the most powerful rulers. The year before he had been presented to Teddy Roosevelt in the White House. Nevertheless, he was a little nervous as he waited for his audience with the king — an audience which the king himself had requested.

Finally the great moment arrived and he was ushered into the presence of His Majesty.

The king was interested in his work of helping the poor and of preaching the Gospel, and this was the subject of their conversation. When their talk was drawing to a close, the king leaned forward and asked him why he had so much zeal for this kind of work.

General Booth smiled at the question, for he had heard it many times. "Some men's passion is art," he said, his black eyes flashing, "some men's passion is fame, some men's passion is gold; but my passion is man."

Before this astounding man had laid down his sword at the time of his "promotion to glory," he had preached sixty thousand sermons, had been introduced to many of the kings of Europe, had received an honorary degree from Oxford University, and had done more than any other man to wrap the golden cable of salvation around the world.

Booth's home in Nottingham, England

Wherever he went, multitudes jammed the largest auditoriums and sat spellbound while he preached about the saving power of the Lord Jesus Christ. But it had not always been this way. There always has to be a beginning, and William Booth's beginning was a discouraging one indeed.

The future general's father, Samuel Booth, finished his breakfast and then pushed his chair away from the table. There was a deep silence in the room, for everyone knew that something important was about to be said. Finally the elder Booth cleared his throat and spoke. "The bank has foreclosed on my last piece of property. I signed a note for a friend, and since he has not been able to pay it, I am held responsible. This means that we are ruined. Our money is gone. It also means that you, William, will have to drop out of the academy and go to work."

"What kind of work do you want me to do?" asked his only son, a salty film forming over his black eyes.

"I have arranged for you to become an apprentice to a pawnbroker."

"A pawnbroker!" exclaimed the lad. A vision of poor people coming to him to borrow money on clothes and cheap jewelry came into a focus in his mind.

"Yes, I have arranged for your apprenticeship to a pawnbroker. It is the easiest way to make money I know of, and I want you to learn to make money — lots of money."

"But I want to help people, not make a living out of them," protested William.

His father did not answer, for he had already left the house.

Going to work at thirteen, while other boys continued their studies and then shouted at play, was not much fun — especially for a boy of William's temperament. His appren-

11

ticeship was to last at least six, and maybe seven, years. And, although he had to work from twelve to sixteen hours a day, he received little pay.

At night when he would get home from the hateful shop he was so tired he would fall asleep without removing his clothes. Sometimes during the night he would dream of the dreadful things that had happened during the day. His master could shrug his shoulders at the money he made from people's misery, but he could not. The high interest William Booth had to collect made him feel like a thief.

His home town of Nottingham was not the gay place legend says it was when it was the headquarters of the bold sheriff who plagued Robin Hood and his merry men. Instead, it was a place of terrible poverty.

Wellington's defeat of Napoleon at Waterloo had brought to a close a series of wars, but it had also opened the doors to long depression. The government had to pay for the war through taxes, and so the taxes were raised until the people groaned under the load. The price of bread was a shilling and two pence for a quarter-loaf, and tea sold for eight shillings a pound. Unskilled laborers who were required to work from fourteen to sixteen hours a day frequently only earned ten shillings a week. In other words, it would take a week's wages to buy a pound of tea and a quarter-loaf of bread!

Wagon loads of children were sent to Nottingham from London and other towns to work in the cotton mills. Some of these children were only six years old and yet they had to spend twelve hours a day in the mill. Many of them barely knew what it was to play!

In every city, and especially in Nottingham, there were thousands of men out of work. The owners of the mills refused to hire adults when they could get the work of children for next to nothing. So poor were the people in these places that it was not uncommon for a dozen people to sleep in one room. There were twenty thousand people in the city of Leeds who received only one shilling a week — not enough to buy a quarter-loaf of bread!

Drunkenness was extremely common. There were thousands of beer shops. A law had been passed so that anyone could buy for two guineas a license to sell beer. Agents went up and down the country getting people to open beer shops. If they didn't have the money to buy the license or even the beer, the brewers provided it on credit. Hundreds of people set up bars in their living rooms and even in kitchens. Sidney Smith, a famous author of the day, wrote, "Everybody is drunk. Those who are not singing are sprawling."

As William trudged home over the spittle-laden streets and saw the drunkenness and poverty, a fire began to burn within him. Something had to be done to help people better their lives. Something simply *had* to be done!

Nottingham was a town where people had always had strong feelings. They were generally "agin" something, especially the government. When Henry VIII closed the monasteries, the people were for the monasteries; in the days of Queen Elizabeth, they had fought against Protestantism; and now with poverty and corruption in high places, they were against the government with all their hearts.

Seldom has a government been more corrupt than it was then. In some places no one could vote unless they owned property. In other places no one could vote but city officials! The country was controlled by a few rich men, and the poor didn't like it. They began to grumble about voting and to demand that reforms be passed that would help them.

Soon those who were not satisfied formed themselves into a stormy group called the "Chartists." The Chartists

13

held big public meetings, published newspapers with flaming stories which criticized the government. They demanded that all men be allowed to vote. As William Booth listened to their leaders, he was spellbound. They had the solution to England's ills, he thought. As soon as possible he joined up with them and did what he could to push forward the cause. Though dog-tired from work, he was never too weary to help in a Chartist meeting. He forced himself to attend even when it was hard to keep his eyes open. He would have given his life for the movement if necessary, for he had already made up his mind that his place in the world was to help the poor.

Soon the leaders decided that they would take a petition to the House of Commons. The petition would demand rights for the poor, and they were determined that they would get a million signatures so the petition could not be ignored by the members of Parliament.

Then someone made the suggestion that after the petition was ready, it should be placed in a cart and dramatically wheeled to the House of Commons by an army of a million men.

When the news of these plans reached the officials, the Duke of Wellington hired a quarter of a million policemen to cope with the expected crowd.

All of this so excited William he could hardly sleep. Every spare moment was spent at the meetings or in getting signatures. Then he began to see that not all the corruption was in the government. Some of the Chartist leaders were vile and wicked men. When they couldn't get people to sign the document, they forged their names. They even copied down names from old gravestones and from out-of-date city directories. He also discovered that many who signed the petition signed it in fun, making up names. One man signed

14

his name as the Duke of Wellington, another as Pug Nose, and another as "Bread and Cheese." This knowledge made him heartsick.

When the great day came, there were only two hundred thousand signatures and only thirty thousand people to wheel the cart to the House of Commons. William was so disappointed, he stayed at home. He remembered how a cousin had told him that the only way to get peace was to accept power from the outside, and now he began to think that this was so.

Late one night as he stumbled home from work, his mother met him at the door. There were tears in her eyes and she cautioned him to be quiet. "Your father is very sick," she said in a hoarse whisper.

He tiptoed into his father's room and found him groaning in pain. Although poor, Samuel Booth had always done what he could for the children. It had never been easy keeping things going when he was well, but now he was confined to bed and things looked hard indeed. William had three sisters, and they could help with the house work. The living, however, now depended on him — and he was only an apprentice. There was only one solution to the problem and that was his father *must* get well.

As the days went by, Samuel Booth sank lower and lower. Each evening as soon as his work was over, William hurried home to enquire about his father, but each time his mother would shake her head and say, "He's much worse."

He felt that if he lost his father, everything would be gone. Although he had been sprinkled as a child, he had not gone to church. Nevertheless, he felt a deep urge to pray for his father, and he did so as he walked the streets of Nottingham. There were days in which his father seemed to improve, but the improvement never lasted. Soon it became evident that he could not live. William dropped into church services, but they were uninteresting and he thought little of them.

Then his father, feeling that the end was near, summoned a friend to teach him about religious things. This man had been converted in a Wesleyan Church and he preached Jesus Christ to the dying man. Samuel Booth accepted Jesus as his personal Saviour and then passed away.

The death of William's father was a staggering blow. Soon the family became so poor they lost their home and had to move to Goose Gate, one of the very poor sections of Nottingham. The little house was right across the street from a slaughter house, and the smell was sometimes almost more than they could endure. His mother made the front

John Wesley

room into a tiny store where she sold needles and thread and other small things. Her sales were very small, but she faced poverty bravely and refused to grumble.

William now began to think more and more about religious matters. He had seen a sense of peace settle over his father when he accepted Christ. Although disappointed in the formal church in which he had been baptized, he began to feel that perhaps there was something to Christianity after all.

When he was fifteen, he started to attend Wesley Chapel in Nottingham. The worship here was not as dry as it had been at the other church, but it was not as warm and full of zeal as it had been forty years before in the days of the flaming John Wesley. As he sat under the Gospel, he longed for someone to talk to him about the way of salvation. But the people were either not interested enough or too timid. Nevertheless, he attended, and the Holy Spirit spoke to his heart. Then one evening he stood to his feet and confessed Christ as his personal Saviour.

On that wonderful day he realized that he would have to make some things right. A while before, through an act of dishonesty, he had received a silver pencil set. He was tempted to say nothing about it, for he had not been discovered. But the Holy Spirit prompted him to go the full way, and so he called the young fellow he had wronged and confessed his sin.

His guilty burden left him immediately. He joined the church and went his way rejoicing. Then he began to feel a great urge to lead others to Christ.

Chapter Two

A Hard Road

WITHIN A FEW HOURS OF HIS CONVERSION, he was out telling the story of Jesus to his friends. He spoke so earnestly of his new happiness that a number of people listened with great interest and a few even promised to go to church. A short time later he gathered a large group of ragged boys from the slums and marched them down to the Wesleyan Church. His little congregation, many of whom had never been inside a church, walked through the main doors and sat down in the first available pews. Although his friends were a little dirty, he felt certain the pastor would be happy with what he had done.

The pastor, however, was very irate about the whole thing. "The next time you want to bring such people here," he scolded, "bring them in through the back door, and seat them where they will not be seen!"

Such a rebuke would have discouraged some, but it didn't phase William Booth. It merely challenged him to work harder. He began to attend cottage prayer meetings, and when the people saw his earnestness, they asked him to lead them. This he always did. When a friend gave him a copy of Charles Finney's *Lectures on Revivals,* he studied it eagerly. He still had to work from seven in the morning until seven at night; but he had forty minutes off for lunch, and during the lunch period he studied the book on revivals. Sometimes he got so interested he forgot to eat.

Frequently he was called to preach at some village

church. He was always glad for these opportunities even though they often meant that he had to trudge home through many miles of darkness and mud. The time came when Dr. Dunn, the pastor of the Wesleyan Church in Nottingham, wanted someone to preach for him in the country. He mentioned his need to the janitor, and the janitor recommended William Booth.

Dunn summoned William to his study and asked him if he thought he could preach. This was the opportunity young Booth had been waiting for and so he replied, "Yes, I think I can preach. I have been preaching for quite a while."

At this the pastor raised an eyebrow and with a sour look on his scholarly face asked, "And who gave you permission to preach?"

William squirmed under his gaze. He had not known that he should ask permission of his pastor to proclaim the saving power of the Lord Jesus Christ. But he respected authority and he respected Dr. Dunn, so he said nothing.

As the years of his apprenticeship crept by, he filled every moment he could with Bible study, preaching, or something that would help him to become a minister. He felt certain that God had called him to become a lay preacher and that salvation would help the poor more than anything else.

Finally the long-looked-forward-to day came. His apprenticeship was over! But the completion of the hated course did not bring the satisfaction he thought it would bring, for now he was faced with the problem of getting a job and earning a living for his widowed mother — and jobs were scarce. There were thousands of unemployed.

Dr. Dunn asked him if he would not enter the full-time ministry. Booth was not sure about this. He had felt a call to preach on Sundays, but he was not sure if the Lord wanted him to spend the whole week in the ministry. "I w-would like to," he stammered, "but I'm only nineteen and my health isn't any too good."

So the pastor sent him to a doctor for a physical examination.

As he sat in the doctor's waiting room, he became convinced that he should, indeed, enter full-time ministerial work. He now chided himself for having suggested to his pastor that he take a physical examination. But he didn't have long for this self condemnation, for he was promptly summoned into the presence of the physician. The doctor gave him various tests and then shook his head. "You are a very nervous boy. If you had the chest of a prize fighter and the constitution of an ox, I'd say go ahead — but since you don't, I wouldn't try."

Booth's eyes filled with tears. "Don't say that to Dr. Dunn," he said.

"But it's the truth! . . ."

"I know," returned Booth, "but I do want so much to preach. Why don't you delay your decision for a year?"

"Well, I guess there could be no harm in that," said the doctor. "In the meantime, be careful, and if you have any trouble come to me immediately."

Happy with this turn of events, he waited around Nottingham for a whole year, preaching when he could and waiting for a job. But waiting for a job did him no good. There were no jobs. The wolf came very close to their door, and there were times when it seemed there would be nothing to eat. He decided that his best course was to go to London. So he kissed his mother good-by and headed for the big city. His sister Ann had married a wealthy Nottingham boy and moved to London. He was certain she would take him in until he found work.

But when he got to the great city he found that Ann's husband was very cold to him and that he could not expect the slightest help from her or her husband.

Penniless and out on the street, he frequently went hungry while he searched for employment. Jobless people were everywhere, and there was as much drunkenness and poverty as in Nottingham — and perhaps a little more. The churches were cold and for the most part appealed only to the rich. Few of them had prayer meetings, and what prayer meetings were conducted were poorly attended. William Booth had never been quite as discouraged as he was then. But he hoped and prayed and had faith that God would make a way for him.

At his wit's end, he finally accepted a job with a pawnbroker in Walworth, a suburb of London. The owner of the place had an apartment above the shop and he allowed William Booth to stay in one of the rooms. But he was as strict about his apartment as he was about the interest he collected. He closed the door at ten o'clock at night, and if his young worker wasn't in by that time, he had to sleep outside!

Booth had only been with him a short time when he started preaching on the streets. Sometimes when there were seekers, he had to suddenly excuse himself and run all of the way home, for having to spend the night on a park bench wasn't very pleasant. But the more opposition he had, the more he studied the Word; and the more he studied the Word, the braver he became.

Having to get home early was not his only problem. A lot of people who heard him said that he could never preach and that God had never called him. One man de-

clared, ". . . there is too much of the shroud in your preaching." Another said, "You are not sufficiently argumentative.
Your sermons do not display sufficient marks of study!"

Many times he returned home weary and beaten. Since
many had told him that he had no ability, he often wondered if God had really called him. And then he would
see the poverty about him and take courage. Of this period
in his life, he later wrote: "How can anybody with spiritual
eyesight talk of having no call, when there are such multitudes around him who never hear a word about God, and
never intend to; who can never hear, indeed, without the
sort of preacher who will force himself upon them?"

Hating the pawnbroking business with all his heart
and feeling that he should be giving all his time to the
Lord's work, he applied to the superintendent of the Wes-
leyans for an opening. But to his great amazement this man,
who controlled a number of churches, replied that there
were no openings and that "preachers are not wanted."

A blow in the face with brass knuckles would not have
shocked him more. He saw the tremendous need for new
churches, for street meetings, for ministers to visit the convicts in the crowded prisons. Everyday he saw hundreds
of people who had probably never heard the story of Jesus.

He looked into the superintendent's face to see if he
were not joking; but the stern lines of the man's face were
hard. There was not the trace of a smile on his lips.

Utterly discouraged, he toyed with the idea of leaving
England. There were ships loaded down with convicts on
their way to Australia. He considered getting a job as a
chaplain on one of these. He took the matter to the Lord
in prayer, and the Lord showed him that he was needed in
England.

22

At that time there was a strong agitation in the Wesleyan Church. Booth stayed out of it, hoping that time would heal the difficulty. But as the days passed by, the difficulty grew. Finally there was a split, and about one third of the churches separated from the main body and formed a group of their own.

Wanting to be as peaceful as possible, William refused to preach in the churches that had split off. But the Wesleyan superintendent, knowing his zeal, decided that he must be one of the reformers and so refused to give him his membership ticket. Hearing what had happened, the split-off churches voted that he become one of them and invited him to preach a sermon in one of their pulpits. And this he did, speaking on the text, "This is indeed the Christ, the Saviour of the world."

A Mr. Rabbitts, a wealthy layman who owned several shoe stores, was in the audience and enjoyed the message very much. He invited the young preacher to dinner and as they walked along he asked, "Why don't you become a minister?"

Booth replied that that was exactly what he wanted to become. Then he named all of the obstacles that had been thrown in his way.

Rabbitts smiled. "God has called you to preach, and you'll have to obey." He walked on for a few steps and then he asked abruptly, "How much money would you have to have each week to make ends meet?"

Booth, not knowing whether he was hearing right or not, replied, "I think I could get by on twelve shillings a week."

Rabbitts stopped and looked at his friend. "Nonsense!" he cried. "No one can live on twelve shillings a week. I'm going to start you out on a pound a week. I'll pay you that much myself for three months."

William Booth

Catherine Booth

Twenty shillings a week sounded like a fortune to William. He agreed to the proposition at once. As he sat at the table with Mr. Rabbitts, his near ministry would have been all he could think about except for the fact that there had been a young lady in the service by the name of Catherine Mumford. She had sat motionless in the congregation and he had noticed her great interest. He wasn't sure whether all her interest had been in the message or in the preacher!

With the promised salary in mind, he gave up his job, rented two rooms in Walford for five shillings a week and bought a few pieces of furniture. He dreamed of a great work at Binfield House, and he was glad to note that Catherine and her mother were enthusiastic members of the congregation.

Catherine and her mother, however, were about the only ones in the group who thought much of his preaching. The others declared that he was an impostor and was not needed. They wondered why they should have a pastor when there were so many lay preachers in the congregation. It was a waste of money to pay a man a salary when there were many preachers who were anxious to preach free of charge!

Rabbitts had only promised to pay him for three months, so when this time was up he was out of a job. With nothing to do and no income, he was forced to sell his furniture for what he could get and live on the proceeds.

The dream he had had of becoming a useful preacher had now been exploded in a million pieces — and the worst of it was that it had happened in Catherine's own congregation. What would the people in Nottingham think when they learned he had lasted only three months!

The money from the furniture didn't last long. In a

25

few days he had spent it all but a sixpence. He held the bright piece of silver between his fingers and wondered what he should do with it. It was all he had; he knew no one would give him any more money and he had no prospects of getting a job. A sixpence wasn't much, but it would buy him something to eat. As he sat and considered how he should spend it, he thought of a widow whose daughter was dying. Without hesitation, he took it to her and thrust it into her palm. Now he faced the world without a job, without a penny, and with no place to sleep.

He took his New Testament from his pocket and re-read the Sermon on the Mount. Then he promised the Lord he would do whatever He wanted him to do, and asked for an opening.

Within a week he was given a letter inviting him to take charge of a Methodist Circuit. This was just the kind of work he wanted, and on the first Sunday he preached in Spaulding to the largest congregation that had ever come to listen to him. He was a little shy as he started his message, but the Lord spoke through him and a number of people received definite help. Then he went to Donnington, the second church in the circuit, and fourteen people responded to his invitation and accepted Christ. He was so happy it seemed that he was walking on air.

The next preaching service was at Swineshead Bridge. This was a place out in the country where the people were very backward. But again God blessed and six people prayed for salvation.

During this eighteen month period in which Booth preached from church to church in the circuit, he kept up a warm correspondence with Catherine Mumford. Catherine, or Kate, as he called her, kept exhorting him to give his all to the Master. She seldom answered one of his letters without enlarging on this idea. Strange love letters they were! But this was what Booth wanted. He decided that such a person would be the ideal one to inspire him in the Lord's work.

From the moment he had first seen her in the congregation, he had decided that God had made her for him and that sooner or later they would be married. He admired her determination and the way she would not give in even though her stand was unpopular. As he went from church to church proclaiming the Gospel, he saw how a wife could help him. He sharpened his pencil and tried to figure how two could live as cheaply as one. But each time he added the figures, he knew his salary was not enough.

Then he received an important looking letter from the Hinds Street Church in London. With eager fingers he tore it open. It was an invitation to become their pastor. They had fewer members than the churches in his circuit, but they offered a much larger salary!

He wrote a glowing letter to Kate for advice. She replied that he should consider the proposition in the light of the good that he could do and warned that the matter of the increased salary should never enter his mind.

As he read her letter, he smiled. It would take a real man to live with a strong-spirited woman like Catherine Mumford!

Chapter Three

Never!

To resign from the Spaulding Circuit where he had seven hundred and fifty members and to take the London Circuit with only two hundred members was quite an act of bravery. The new group did offer more money, but would they be able to pay it? He had won two hundred souls the year before in the other churches. Would the people in London respond as well? He had heard many preachers say that London was the graveyard of evangelists.

With some misgiving, he decided he would make the change. But the doubts he had about his new work left him after his first sermon, for on that trying day fifteen people made decisions for Christ.

Dr. William Cooke, one of the great preachers of the group, lived in London. A generous soul, he opened up his home to young ministers and taught them. Booth felt that this was a good opportunity for him, and so he arranged to study under the famous leader for six months. This meant that he had a heavy schedule, but he was sure it was worth while.

During the day he sat with his books, but each evening and often three times on Sunday, he was out preaching the Gospel. Everywhere he went great crowds of people came, and he seldom had a service in which someone was not converted.

He kept track of the sermons he preached and the souls that were won. And since he wanted to do as much good

28

as possible, he began to note which kind of a sermon won the most souls. He soon discovered that he was the most successful when he warned the people of the wrath to come. In a letter to Kate we find him saying, "I want a sermon on the Flood, one on Jonah, and one on the Judgment. Send me some bare thoughts; some clear, startling outline. Nothing moves people like the terrific. They must have hell-fire flashed before their eyes or they will not move. Last night I preached a sermon on Christ weeping over sinners, and only one came forward. . . . When I preached about the harvest and the wicked being turned away, numbers came. We must have the kind of truth that will move sinners."

The harder he worked, the more souls he won and the happier he became. Often, instead of studying the books he should have been studying, he was on his knees praying for souls. Feeling bad because he did not make more progress with his books, he took the matter to Dr. Cooke. His teacher smiled, "I have nothing to say to you, Mr. Booth. Go on and may God bless you." This was not hard for him to say, for his own daughter had been saved through Booth's ministry.

After several months of unusually successful meetings, Dr. Cooke took Booth for a walk through his garden. "I intend proposing you at the next Conference as superintendent of the work in London," he said.

"Oh, I could never do that," objected Booth. "I'm not old enough. I don't have enough experience."

"Nonsen e," replied Cooke. "You're just the man we need. You have enthusiasm, and you've had more success than anyone I've ever seen in London."

The two walked along in silence for a bit, and then Booth said, "I don't want to be the superintendent. But I'll be glad to be the assistant."

29

This proposition was suggested to the Conference.

"But how will we pay him?" objected one of the preachers. "The London Circuit has hard enough problems to support one man without trying to support two!"

"If you'll give Booth the job, I'll pay him," said his old friend Mr. Rabbitts.

With such a wide open door, Booth could not refuse, so he became the assistant pastor of the London Circuit. His popularity increased, and it soon became difficult to find buildings that would contain the crowds who were eager to hear him preach.

Reports of his wonderful meetings began to appear in Christian papers throughout the land, and ministers began to write to him asking for campaigns. Booth rejoiced in his progress, for it meant that more souls were being saved. The vast crowds did not turn his head, and he knew that if he ever became conceited, he would be ruined. But the crowds began to bring him another trouble—jealousy. Other ministers of the Gospel just could not stand his success and prosperity.

He never dreamed that one person could become envious of another in the great task of soul-winning. He tried to refuse to take any meetings outside his own circuit, but some of the invitations were so pressing he could not resist. One of the first of these was at Bristol. Here they had an unusually fine meeting and a number were saved. Then he went to Guernsey with even greater success.

His fame had now spread to Hanley — the home of the potteries. Here there was a very large congregation with one of the largest chapels in the world. When he was invited to come, he shrank from the honor. The building was too big. The people were used to great preachers. He was just a young man. But the congregation refused to take "no" for an answer. They wanted Booth for a revival meeting and they were going to have him!

When he complained that he had been neglecting his own circuit, they went to the conference and got permission for him to stay with them an entire month. Still he hesitated. But Kate told him that he should go — and after much prayer he concluded that it was the will of the Lord. He packed his grips and bought a ticket for Hanley.

On Sunday, January 14, he got up from his seat and stepped out to face one of the largest congregations he had ever seen. He had wondered how these solemn people would take to his style of preaching. But before he had uttered a dozen words he knew they were with him. As always, he preached from the depth of his heart and they stayed with him. They laughed when he laughed. They cried when he cried. By the end of the meeting nearly five hundred decided for Christ. It was a great triumph for the son of a bankrupt father and a former pawnbroker's helper.

He wrote to Kate about his success and she was delighted, but she wrote him urging that he not get puffed up and that he continue to give his all to the Master.

From Hanley he went to Burslem and then to Mossley; from there to Newcastle-under-Lyme and then to other places. At the end of four months there were 1,739 people who had sought salvation. As he and Kate thought about all of this, they were sure that God had called them to evangelistic work.

Their engagement was now definite. They were certain that God had meant them for each other. Their only delay in getting married was to wait for the proper time. Finally they settled on a date, June 16, 1855.

Dr. Thomas performed the ceremony at the Stockwell

New Chapel. It was a quiet wedding with few people present. Kate and William wanted it this way. They felt that it was wrong to waste money on elaborate ceremonies when there were so many hungry people in the world.

The moment they had taken their vows, they went to Ryde on the Isle of Wight. They stayed here a week and then sailed for Guernsey where they planned to be quiet and enjoy a honeymoon. But their plans had been discovered and when they got there they found the pier thronged with people who planned for them to conduct a revival meeting!

So great were the crowds that came that it was necessary to open the doors of the church at five-thirty so the regular members could get in before the crush. Night after night the building was jammed to the doors with people sitting or standing in every possible place. Some even sat on the rafters.

The excitement proved to be more than Kate could bear, and during some of the services she had to remain in their room in bed.

At the conclusion of the revival, they sailed to York for another meeting. But the voyage was too much for Kate. She became so ill she had to return to her mother while William went ahead with the meeting by himself.

The Booths were extremely happy with evangelistic work, even though it frequently meant separation. Booth, especially, liked the big crowds and the satisfaction of seeing hundreds of people saved. The Conference was now arranging his slate, and he felt that the leaders of the group were satisfied with his work and wanted him to continue. When the Annual Conference met in 1857 he felt that it was not necessary for him to be present. He believed the preachers would remember how the Lord was blessing him and would ask him to continue in evangelistic work.

Imagine his surprise, then, when he learned that J. P. Wright, the superintendent of the Nottingham circuit, had led a fight against him, with the result that he would be asked to give up evangelism and take charge of a circuit. At first he couldn't believe it. But when he checked with a friend who had been present, he learned that it was so. The Conference had debated the issue for five hours, and that was their startling conclusion!

When Kate heard this, she was in bed ill. She was so thoroughly disgusted she wanted to break away from the Conference immediately and work for the Lord in some other field. William, however, didn't agree with her. He felt that in time the preachers would see that God had called him to be an evangelist and not pastor a circuit.

Many laymen wrote to him begging him to continue on his own. One man said, "Oh, Brother Booth, if I could preach and floor the sinners as you can, I would not thank Queen Victoria to be my aunt or cousin! When I hear or read of your success, I could wish to be your shoe-black!" This was very flattering indeed, but Booth did not want to cause trouble. He agreed to take a circuit.

They moved to the smoky town of Brighouse, and there their second son was born. They named him Ballington. Their first son, Bramwell, had been born in Halifax on March 8, 1856.

Booth felt like a bird with its wings clipped. It was extremely hard to be content preaching to hundreds when he knew he could be preaching to thousands. But whenever Kate grumbled about their work, he assured her that they must be patient and that everything would work out all right.

With great hopes that he would be loosed for evangelistic work, Booth attended the next annual conference at Hull. But again the preachers shook their heads at his request and assigned him to a circuit. This time his headquarters were at Gateshead.

Gateshead had a building that seated nearly 2,000 but the membership was very small. The first time he preached there he preached mostly to empty seats. But he and his wife got busy and soon the building was packed to the doors and people were standing in the aisles. Indeed, they had so much success the people began to call their church "the converting shop."

When Booth talked of going into evangelistic work toward the close of the first year in Gateshead, the people raised a storm. They insisted that he stay with them. This he promised to do. But since he always wanted to do more than he was doing, he started preaching on the streets.

He would line up those of his congregation who would attend and get them to march through the streets while they sang Gospel songs. Frequently they were laughed at and even stoned, but this did not discourage Booth.

Kate went from door to door visiting and helping the poor and urging the people to sign a pledge not to drink. She soon discovered poverty that she had never dreamed existed. She threw her all into the work.

They labored in Gateshead for three years. Each time they hoped the Annual Conference would allow them to return to evangelistic work, but each time they were turned down. As the third conference drew near, Booth wrote a long letter to one of the leaders explaining why he wanted to give up the circuit for revival meetings. He felt confident that this man would help him.

When the great day for the meeting came, William and

Catherine stood up and called out, "Never, William, never!"

Kate went together, each one praying that the Conference would at last allow them to do the thing for which God had called them.

When he entered the building, Booth was told that his future would be settled then and there. Dr. Cooke gave him a reassuring smile and promised to do the best he could for him. Finally the subject came up. Those who opposed his evangelistic work declared that it was an insult for a pastor to have to call in an evangelist. For, they declared, it was a reflection on the pastor's ministry, indicating that he could not get the people saved himself.

The argument went back and forth for a long time. Then Dr. Cooke got up and suggested a compromise. He said that it would be a good thing to send Booth back to a circuit, but with the strict understanding that he be allowed to go out and conduct several revival meetings each year.

Booth had feared that it might be this way. He knew that it would not work. He felt that he would either have to be an evangelist or a pastor; to do both would be impossible.

William remained silent as the verdict they expected was read. This verdict was that they should be given a circuit with the privilege of conducting a few revivals each year. He respected authority and did not want to cause trouble. But the whole thing was more than Kate could stand. She got up from her seat in the front row of the gallery and, facing her husband, said in a loud clear voice that everyone could hear, "Never, William, never!"

Her tones had the note of finality in them.

Booth waved his hat toward the door, indicating that she should meet him there. At the door he embraced her and then stepped out onto the street, without a friend and without a farthing. They knew that their actions would mean that ministers would be afraid to call them for meetings and that their salary would be immediately stopped. There were four children to feed, but they didn't worry. They *knew* God was leading them!

Chapter Four

Revival in a Graveyard

THE BOOTHS HEADED FOR THE HOME where they were stay-
ing during the Conference. Both of them had hoped that
such a scene would never take place, even though Kate
had declared that it could not be avoided.

They had barely stepped into the living room when
there was a loud knock at the door. "See who it is, William," said Kate, as she sank wearily into a chair.

Booth opened the door to face his old friend, Dr.
Cooke.

"I have come," said the distinguished gentleman, "to
see if I can't help the situation." He strode confidently
across the room. He had helped patch up things before,
and by the earnestness in his face it appeared that he felt
he could help again. "We need you in the Conference.
There aren't many who can preach as well as you can.
Don't let us down!"

"But we want to do evangelistic work. That is our
call," said Kate firmly.

"I know, I know," returned Dr. Cooke kindly, "but you
have patience with other people. Have patience with the
Conference. . . ."

"We've had patience with them long enough," inter-
rupted Kate. "Each year it's the same. They just don't
want us to do what God has called us to do. If John Wesley were here . . . ."

"Maybe we'd better go along with them for another

38

The tent had been erected in an old burial ground

year," said Booth reluctantly. He was remembering his many fine friends in the Conference and that Paul had exhorted Christians to be patient.

Kate didn't want to agree, and after a period of soul-searching William gave in to her wishes. This was a decision he never regretted. Kate was usually right, and he was the first to admit it!

The circuit offered to them was one of the most run-down circuits in England. But this was not the reason they turned it down. They turned it down because they felt that that was God's will. Booth had learned, very early in his ministry, that God's ways are not human ways; and that it always pays to listen to Him.

Finally, he made up his mind and moved to London. They moved to the great city purely on faith. And a great deal of faith it was, too; there were four children to feed, and because of his bold stand there were no calls for revivals.

They selected a home in London and moved in. When the children asked what they were going to do, Kate replied, "We're going to work for the Lord." But at the time there were no open doors to the Lord's work. They felt sure, however, that God had work for them, and that He would supply their needs.

Then they received an invitation to hold a meeting in a tent that had been erected in an old burial ground. They were called because the expected evangelist had become ill. The prospects for a fruitful meeting in this place were dim indeed, but it was an opening and they decided to take it.

The poor East-enders thronged to the tent

The location was among the poorest of the poor. Drunks and tramps were all over the streets. But when the Booths saw them, they loved them and later William Booth wrote about this experience. "When I saw those masses of poor people, so many of them without God or hope in the world, and found that they so readily and eagerly listened to me, following from open-air meeting to tent, and accepting, in many instances, my invitation to kneel at the Saviour's feet there and then, my whole heart went out to them. I walked back to our West End home and said to my wife:

"'O Kate, I have found my destiny! These are the people for whose salvation I have been longing all these years. As I passed by the doors of the flaming gin-palaces tonight I seemed to hear a voice sounding in my ears, "Where can you go and find such heathen as these, and where is there so great a need of your labors?" And there and then in my soul I offered myself and you and the children up to this great work. Those people shall be our people, and they shall have our God for their God.'"

The poor East-enders thronged to the tent. Many of them accepted Christ. Booth wrote an article about his experiences to *The Christian* and we quote part of it here: "I have been engaged in an effort in this direction for the last six weeks. Invited by Messrs. Stabb and Chase, I held a week's service in a large tent erected in the Quakers' burying ground, Thomas Street, Whitechapel. So evident was the divine approval that the services have been continued until now. Nearly every night two meetings are held, first an open-air on the Mile-End Road, and afterwards in the tent. On the last two Sabbaths we have conducted four services each day. . . .There have been but two or three meetings at which sinners have not professed to find mercy, and sometimes thirteen or fourteen have come forward of an evening. . . .

"We have no definite plans. We wish to be guided by the Holy Spirit. At present we desire to hold consecutive services for the purpose of bringing souls to Christ in different localities of East London all the year around. We propose to hold these meetings in halls, theatres, chapels, tents, open-air, and elsewhere, as the way may be opened, or as we seem likely to attain the end we have in view. . . .

"In order to carry on this work, we intend to establish a 'Christian Revival Association,' in which we think a hundred persons will enroll themselves at once. We shall also require some central building in which to hold more private meetings, and in which to preach the Gospel when not engaged in special work elsewhere.

"To work out these plans it will manifest to each reader of this that funds will be required, and to those whom the Lord has entrusted with means, and who have any sympathy with the perishing thousands for whom this work is organized, we appeal for help."

Booth hoped that some of the readers of the article would take it seriously and send some money. Trying to get enough money from the people to whom he preached would have been impossible. Those who were saved were glad to give, but most of them were on the verge of starvation and had nothing.

When the article came out, William showed it to his wife. "Now pray, Kate," he said, "that someone with money will read this and get a vision of what we've seen."

The two of them knelt together and pled with God that He would make it possible for them to continue this kind of work.

Soon a letter was handed to them bearing the return

43

address of Samuel Morely. As Booth looked at the name, he wondered who it could be. There was a Samuel Morely who was a member of Parliament, but surely he would not write to a poor Gospel preacher working in the slums of East London!

With trembling fingers he tore the envelope open and took out the letter. Then his black eyes swam with tears. The letter was from Samuel Morely, M.P. And in it the distinguished member of Parliament said that as soon as he got back from Scotland he wanted to learn more about their work and that he expected to help them!

William and Kate could barely believe their eyes. His money and his influence would really be a help. They got on their knees and thanked God for his blessing.

But their elation was just for a day. On the third Sunday after he'd promised to give his life to the East-enders, he went to the burial ground to preach and found that a wind had blown the tent down. Quickly he examined it. Then he rose to his feet, shaking his head. The cloth was old and had been ripped in many pieces. It could not be repaired!

There was only one thing to do and that was to find another place to meet. He went from building to building, looking for a place for his converts to worship. But in each place the owner shook his head. Again he and his wife got on their knees and prayed that God would show them a way. Then they discovered a large dance hall. He shuddered at the thought of preaching in such a place.

"You could never have services here," said Kate, sweeping her eyes over the large bare floor. "Look at the dirt. And where would the people sit?"

"We could get the chairs from the graveyard and have them in place for Sunday morning," returned William.

"But they have a big dance Saturday night. There wouldn't be time. . . ."

"There will be time if we start early enough," replied Booth grimly.

He hated to ask the people to help him move the benches, especially the new converts. But he went to them with his story and they responded bravely. But in order to get everything ready on time, it was necessary for them to get up and start to work by four o'clock in the morning. And then, after the evening service, they had to take the seats out again! Fortunately they discovered an old shed where discarded rags had been stored to hold their mid-week service in, and so didn't have to work so hard to prepare for it.

At first Booth wondered if the people would be willing to help. But he soon discovered that they were not only glad to work hard for the organization, but that they grew spiritually when they had something to do.

There were times when he had to turn his face because of the stench of their clothes. But the love of Christ gleaming in their eyes warmed his heart and made him know that the sacrifice was worth all the effort he could put forth.

There were other troubles in the dance hall besides the problem of bringing in and taking out the chairs. The owner of the place, greedy for money, used the building on Sundays as a photographer's studio. In order to get into the auditorium, the congregation had to pass through a room in which a woman sat touching up photographs.

The boys in the neighborhood of the shed where the prayer meetings were held amused themselves by throwing firecrackers through the opened windows. Even in the summer when it was terribly hot, Booth had to keep the windows closed to escape the firecrackers.

Thinking they could better themselves, they moved from the dance hall to a horse stable. But they were soon told to move from here because their meetings disturbed a school on the other side of the wall. Then they moved to an amusement hall. But this didn't work out and they were forced into an old beer house, the Eastern Star. Here they were annoyed by gangs of hoodlums. These hoodlums would sing vulgar songs in front of the door. When this didn't move the congregation, they started blowing horns and pounding on cans. During the winter, they burned foul smelling things near the ventilators in order to make the people cough and so break up the meeting. When Booth appealed to the police, they merely smiled and shrugged their shoulders.

Years later, thinking of these days, Booth declared, "The day has gone when the priest and the Levite are content to pass by the wounded man. They must needs stop now, turn back, and punch the head of any good Samaritan who dares come to the rescue."

During these trying days, some of Booth's followers began to grumble about his preaching. They declared that he preached far too much on repentance. When they went to him, asking that he let up on the subject, he refused. "As long as repentance is in the Bible," he affirmed, pointing to a tattered copy on the table, "I'm going to preach repentance."

"In that case we'll have to leave you and go to another church," said a spokesman.

Booth knew he would miss them. His load at the moment was very heavy. But he shook his head. "I'll miss you," he said, forcing himself to smile. "You are my friends.

46

But since Peter preached repentance and since it's all through the New Testament, I'll have to preach it, too."

They pled with him again. But he had made up his mind, and so they left him to struggle alone.

Opportunity now came to rent a theatre on Sundays. The rent, however, was high. And now with many of their people gone, they had even less money. But as great as the rent was, their faith was even greater. He and Kate went to their knees and stayed there until they felt assured that God would help them.

About a month after they had received their first letter from Samuel Morely, they received another inviting William Booth to meet him for an interview.

Fortified with prayer, Booth called on Mr. Morely. He knew the author of the two letters was interested, but he wasn't sure if he was interested enough to help them in a financial way. From bitter experience he knew that words are cheap, and that "there is many a slip between the cup and the lip."

Morely met him with an outstretched hand and directed him to a chair in his comfortable office. He then questioned him closely about his work and about the methods being used. He asked him to outline what he wanted to do in the future and how he expected to do it.

Encouraged by this enthusiasm, Booth related his dream of helping the East-enders. He explained that he felt their greatest help was salvation — that this alone would rescue them from drink. He also said that they needed friends, understanding friends who would love them in spite of their rags. "There are many people who are down, Mr. Morely, but none of them are out!"

He was talking about the needs of the people when

47

Morely suddenly whipped out a check. "What are your own personal needs?" he demanded.

When Booth hesitated he said, "Tell me the number of children you have, and what it costs to keep your place going."

He had not gone to talk about his own needs, but his host kept after him, so he finally gave in. Morely smiled, filled out the check and as he handed it to him said, "This is for the needs of your family. I'll send you some more later. You are doing a great work. Keep it up. I'm behind you."

Booth was so happy he praised God all the way home.

Chapter Five

Forward March

THE EFFINGHAM THEATRE HAD HAD a bad reputation for a long time, but it was a big building and was located among the kind of people Booth wanted to reach. He rented the place on faith. Soon it was filled and scores of people were saved every Sunday within its worldly walls. The news of this success reached the Evangelization Society of London. They sent a committee to investigate. Mr. Bewley from Dublin had given the society five thousand pounds to help the spiritual condition of the poor. The committee came back from Booth's meetings with a glowing report. After a quick conference, word was sent to Booth that the Evangelization Society would pay the rent at the theatre. This was a definite victory.

He preached here until he was able to build a bigger and better building in Whitechapel. This new building cost thirty-five hundred pounds, seated twelve hundred people and had a bookstore in the front. There were also rooms upstairs for offices and private meetings.

On a Sunday evening as many as ten speakers would go into different sections of the area and gather a group of people, then march the group to the building where they would hear the Gospel. Frequently as they marched along they would be hooted and stoned by the mob, but the leaders didn't mind, for they knew they were working for the Lord.

Although these people were poor, Booth knew it was

best for them to at least help support the work. Frequently, just before the collection, he would say, "You used to give three or four shillings a week for beer and tobacco before you were converted, and we shall not be content with a penny a week or a shilling a week. Give as the Lord has prospered you, and down with the money."

As soon as this place was going, Booth decided to open a branch in Shoreditch, another wretched part of London. Here it was as hard to find a place to meet as it had been in the East End. In desperation, Booth agreed to take a place behind a "pigeon-shop." G. S. Railton described it well: "The pigeon-shop, filled with pet birds and animals of all descriptions, and always as full of the peculiar stench which such places alone produce, was as dirty and disagreeable a spot as one could well imagine, although the people who kept it were so much in their element that they lived, ate, drank and smoked, and slept in the same apart-

Commissioner G. S. Railton, an early Army chronicler

ment wherein they carried on their business, Sundays and weekdays alike. . . .

"But if you were not inclined for birds or white mice, and passed by these attractions, you would certainly have found something far more wonderful at the end of the little passage and across the yard, where a large pen of fowls kept up a ceaseless chatter. There was a little room, scarcely twenty feet square, lit mainly in the daytime through a little skylight, the low ceilings supported by pillars intended probably to insure the safety of the workshop above. The floor boards were in such a state they gave way sometimes beneath our feet; the drainage was defective; and in summer the room was almost unendurably hot. Nevertheless, whoever will receive the testimony of those who knew the place best, will, we are sure, be satisfied that in this little place God Almighty wrought wonders such as the power of His Spirit alone can accomplish."

Perhaps Booth would rather have had a better place, but he had already learned that the poor would rather come to such a hovel than to enter a church. At any rate the work here prospered!

In these days it was not his desire to start an independent organization. He merely wanted to get the people saved and then to send them to the regular churches. But he soon found that this would not work, for the churches, in many cases, did not want them; and the people did not want the churches. He also discovered that he had a strong affection for the people and he wanted them himself.

He believed very strongly that all converts — even though they were drunken wretches and their clothes were in the pawnshop when they were saved — should work for the Lord. Among the first things he asked a new convert to do was to testify. Sometimes this took a little persuasion, for most of them had never been before the public. But testify they did, and what remarkable testimonies they were! Many had been drunkards, some had been thieves; others had beaten their wives. One man testified that he had sold his child's coffin for drink; another, that he had robbed a store.

People from the large churches who came to listen often shuddered at the terrible tales they heard. But all of them had to agree that salvation meant everything to those who had been saved.

Soon people from other parts of London demanded that branches be opened in their sections. And this Booth did just as soon as possible. In a very short time there were over a dozen meeting places. At first Booth advertized for leaders to take care of these branches. Some of the leaders who came in this way did very well. But the people wanted leaders who had been like themselves saved from the gutter.

Some said that it would be impossible to make preachers out of former alcoholics, that if he tried it he would run into any number of difficulties. When he declared that he was going to try it anyway, they lifted their hands in horror.

He never lost sight of his mission to help the worst kind of people. "We are moral scavengers," he said, "netting the very sewers. We want all we can get, but we want the lowest of the low." He knew that the leadership that would get this kind of people had to come from the ranks.

Frequently a man would find himself on the platform within a few weeks of his conversion. And sometimes friends who had been away for a while would be startled by the sudden change. Many times these men and women made dreadful mistakes in English and even in doctrine, but the Lord blessed them anyway. Indeed some were qualified by

52

their evil days to answer the crowd in a way others could not have done.

One of the young women was holding a meeting on the street of a large town. A dirty hoodlum walked up to her and said, "What does an ignorant girl like you know about religion? I know more than you do. I can say the Lord's Prayer in Latin."

The young lady smiled and then replied, "I can say more than that. I can say the Lord saved my soul in English." The crowd loved this reply and stayed with her until she was finished.

A rough fisherman who had been saved was preaching to a big crowd of men in London. His sermon was based on the parable of the pounds. When he read the words, "Lord, I feared these because thou art an austere man," he misread the word "austere" as "oyster." He then went on to tell the hard life of oystermen. He explained how they risked their lives, and how they frequently cut their fingers on the sharp rocks. When he was through, he gave an invitation and twelve people went forward seeking salvation.

At the door a man stopped him. "My dear friend," he said, "the word is austere and not oyster."

"Oh, well," replied the old fisherman, "we got a dozen oysters anyway!"

As the work expanded, Booth began to dream of his children giving their lives for it. He praised the work of the Lord in front of them whenever he could and showed them how it was better than any other work. One afternoon he led his oldest boy through the swinging doors of a saloon and, pointing to the men drinking at the crowded bar, said, "These are the people I want you to live and labor for." He said this with so much earnestness the son never forgot it.

53

Anxious that his children have a happy childhood and love his ministry, he did what he could to make them happy. He loved to romp with them on the floor, letting them pull his beard and tie him up.

One afternoon while he was taking his regular nap, his daughter Emma came in and did his hair up in little paper rolls. When she was through, he was a horrible sight, looking like a man from another planet. She had just finished when a servant knocked, saying that there was a visitor downstairs. Booth, not knowing how he looked, started down the steps. Horrified at what would follow, Emma and another sister grabbed his coattails and held him until he could see himself in a mirror!

The boys had a regular menagerie in the back yard. There were rabbits, rats, guinea pigs, and chickens. Booth enjoyed watching the animals as they were fed. He was as proud of them as were the boys. If the rabbit or the rat got sick, he was as concerned as they.

When their eighth and last baby, Lucy, was born, Booth gathered the children around him. Then, in his most solemn tones, he said, "Now listen; I have got a wonderful piece of news for you. God has sent us a most beautiful present."

"Is it alive?" shouted the children together.

"Yes, it's alive."

"Is it a dog?"

"No."

"A donkey?"

"No."

When they were about to give up, he said, "It's a baby."

The children were delighted to hear this and crept upstairs on tiptoes to see what the newcomer looked like. When they saw its little pink face and wisp of hair, they shouted for joy.

Afterwards one of them confessed that he had been praying for a donkey and was a little disappointed!

Miss Short, who spent a Christmas day in their home, tells an interesting story about it. "The General had determined that the children should have a thoroughly old-fashioned Christmas, and for a week beforehand every preparation was made for a great family festival. The children were full of excitement, and their father entered into the spirit of the thing, and I really thought it would be a day of purest happiness. But when the General returned from preaching in Whitechapel on Christmas morning, he was pale, haggard, and morose. He did his best to enter into the children's fun and frolic, but it was no use; he kept relapsing into silence and gloom. He looked dreadfully white and drawn, just as if he were ill or harassed by some grievous worry. And then suddenly he burst out, 'I'll never have a Christmas Day like this again!' and, getting on his feet and walking up and down the room like a caged lion, he told us of the sights he had seen that morning in Whitechapel. . . . 'The poor have nothing but the public-house — nothing but the public-house [saloon]!' "

This was the last time they ever celebrated Christmas at home. From then on they scattered out among the poor to distribute plum puddings! Booth asked the Lord to bless the puddings before they were delivered, and the children had a wonderful time seeing the cheer their gifts brought. One year the Booth family alone made presents of one hundred and fifty puddings. This was the beginning of the famous Salvation Army Christmas Day to which so many of us contribute, dropping our coins into the Army buckets at busy street corners.

Whenever one of the children gave indications that they might want to enter some other line of work, Booth

55

*Evangeline Booth at the age of 14, her deep spirituality
already evident*

would begin to pray that they would change their minds. As a little boy Bramwell decided he wanted to be a surgeon. In order to practice his art, he borrowed Emma's doll so that he could operate on it.

When he cut it open, the sawdust leaked out. This caused Emma to burst into tears.

"Silly child!" cried Bramwell, as he carefully made another incision. "Do you think you can have an operation without blood?"

The work of the Lord under Booth was growing as rapidly as his children, and like them, it had its awkward stages. In the beginning in 1865 the work was called the East London Mission. This was a fine name for it at that time, for all of the work was done in East London. But as the work spread to other parts of London and then to Scotland the name had to be changed. The new name was "Christian Mission."

Less than ten years after the work had started the Booths found that they had over thirty meeting places. There were two hundred and sixty-five lay preachers, and these men and women had conducted ten thousand services in one year! Three thousand people had professed conversion in these meetings, and everyone who had been saved was out working to tell the Good News to others.

Many of his preachers now believed that the work was big enough and that he should stop establishing new places of worship. Tired from his many duties, Booth knew that this was the easy way. And many a man, having done as much as William and Kate, would have been content to rest. But they had seen the poverty of England and Scotland and Ireland, and they had seen the power of the Lord. They frequently were alarmed at the growth and wondered if they could handle any more people. But each time they prayed about it, they came to the conclusion that the Lord was saying, "Forward, march!"

One afternoon as he was returning home, he heard some children singing. He listened closely and soon recognized the words. They were singing an old drinking song, the words of which went:

Up and down the City Road,
In and out the Eagle,
That's the way the money goes,
Pop goes the weasel.

As Booth listened, he quickened his step and angrily clenched his hands until his knuckles were white. He knew the tragic meaning of the crude poem. The City Road led to the Eagle, one of the biggest and worst drinking places in London. This was where many men spent money that should have purchased bread. After their money was gone, they would go to a nearby pawnshop and pawn (pop) their watch (weasel) to get money to buy more beer.

There were some who smiled at the chorus and laughed at the men staggering down the street. But William and Kate Booth were not among them. They got on their knees and wept and prayed.

Chapter Six

The Birth of an Army

WEARING A LONG, YELLOW DRESSING GOWN and felt slippers, Booth paced back and forth in his bedroom dictating to G. S. Railton. "We are a volunteer army," he said.

While Railton was writing this down, young Bramwell Booth leaned back in his chair and exclaimed, "Volunteer! I'm not a volunteer. I'm a regular or nothing!"

William Booth stood still for a long moment, a thoughtful frown on his face. Then he went up to Railton and, leaning over his shoulder, crossed out the word "volunteer," and above it wrote "salvation." The sentence now read, "We are a salvation army." The effect of that phrase, "salvation army," was so startling that Bramwell and Railton jumped out of their chairs. With glowing eyes Bramwell shouted, "Thank God for that!" And so the wonderful name that was to be known to hundreds of millions was born.

Up to this time military terms were only occasionally used. At home Booth was frequently called the "General," for his real title, General Superintendent, seemed too long for the children. And once he had been introduced to a large congregation as the General of the Hallelujah Army.

After the name Salvation Army had been agreed upon, a new letterhead was printed. On the left there was a list of the forty-seven meeting places, and at the top was the name, General William Booth. When Booth saw this he scribbled on the margin, "Can't this form be altered? It looks pretentious."

The name, however, stuck; and soon military terms were being used throughout the organization. No longer was a revival advertized as a mere revival. Armies did not conduct revivals, they launched campaigns! In one city where Booth was to preach, loud placards announced:

THE GENERAL OF THE HALLELUJAH ARMY IS COMING TO REVIEW HIS TROOPS. GREAT BATTLES WILL BE FOUGHT.

At another place, his troops carried banners on which had been written in flaming words:

BOMBARDMENT AND SHELLING OF HECKMONDWICKE. TROOPS WILL ARRIVE SATURDAY NIGHT. FIRST BOM-BARDMENT ON SUNDAY MORNING. FIRST VOLLEY FIRED AT SOUND OF BUGLE AT 10 A.M.

A circular proclaimed dramatically:

GREAT BATTLES WILL BE FOUGHT ON SAND HILL. WAR CHARIOTS AND TEN MOUNTED GUNS. RED-HOT SHOTS WILL BE FIRED NEAR MARKET HALL.

Preachers came to be known as officers, and when a group of them met for discussions, they were regarded and advertized as having "Councils of War." Meeting places were known as "Citadels" or "Outposts." Those who studied to become officers were known as "Cadets." The one second to the General was the Chief of Staff. The beliefs of the Salvation Army were set down as "Articles of War."

With all of these new titles and ideas came new courage. Some of the preachers didn't like the military methods and many of them left the movement; but a great many more came in. Indeed, so many wanted to preach they had to be very careful whom they chose.

Sometimes when a person came to Booth saying he wanted to be an officer, Booth would discourage him by describing the difficulties in the work. If they still wanted to preach after his discouraging talk, they were considered fit material. All of their preachers did not come from the slums. Many cultured people gave up good jobs in order to march with the Salvation Army. One young man who was later known as Commissioner Booth-Tucker gave up his job as a judge in the Indian Civil Service in order to work with the Army. His position as judge paid a thousand pounds a year, but he was more interested in the Gospel than in money.

For a while the new Army did its work in ordinary street clothes. Then someone suggested that uniforms be used. A few objected to the idea, but others said that it would be a fine thing. It would advertize the Salvation Army to the world, and it would increase the respect for the officers.

Kate was the one who designed the famous "Hallelujah bonnet" for the women. She shut herself up in a room with her daughter and examined a big display of bonnets. She wanted something that would be distinctive so that the officer wearing it would be immediately recognized. But she also wanted something attractive. After considerable search and study, they decided on the one that is used today.

The banner under which they marched carried the words "Blood and Fire." The "Fire" stood for the Holy Spirit, and the "Blood" for the blood of the Lord Jesus Christ. One of Booth's favorite texts was, ". . . and without shedding of blood is no remission" (Hebrews 9:22).

Many of the officers were musicians. Soon the towns and cities became accustomed to the Salvation Army as

61

One of the early bands

Today's Chicago Salvation Army Staff Band

they paraded down the streets to the stirring Gospel music of the bands. Frequently the big drum was used as an altar, and there are today hundreds of men and women who were saved while they knelt in front of a big drum on a busy street.

Booth demanded complete loyalty from his troops. No slackers were allowed. Each officer was required to fill out a form indicating what had been done during the day. Anyone convicted of idleness had either to change or get out. Booth's favorite slogan was, "Every hour and every power for Christ and duty."

Sometimes when he was going through a town where they had an outpost, the local officer would meet him at the train.

"How are you getting on here, Captain?" Booth would ask.

If the Captain replied, "Pretty well," Booth would retort, "Go on! You must do better than your best!"

He worked like a horse and didn't see why everyone else should not do the same. Every time he saw a drunkard, or a tramp, or a prisoner, he determined to work harder. One morning Bramwell found him in his room vigorously brushing his hair. "Bramwell," said Booth, an ache in his voice, "did you know that men slept out all night on the bridges?"

His son replied, "Yes, I think that many are sleeping out. There are a lot of poor people in the city."

"Then you ought to be ashamed of yourself to have known it and done nothing for them."

Bramwell pled that they were burdened down already and couldn't possibly help them, regardless of their poverty.

"Go and do something, Bramwell. We must do something," replied Booth, raising his voice.

63

"But that will cost a lot of money," argued Bramwell, for he knew the funds in the treasury were low.

"Well, that is your affair!" replied Booth. "Something must be done. Get hold of a warehouse and warm it, and find something to cover them."

The business of the Salvation Army was to attack all the forces of evil and poverty. And this it did with great success. One would have thought that everyone would have rejoiced, but there were many who did all they could to ruin it.

Some came out to cheer when the Salvation Army band went by; others came with stones and rotten eggs. One year nearly seven hundred officers were molested by the savage bands that fought them. Sometimes Army leaders were arrested under false charges. In 1882 seventy-one men and fifteen women were locked up in jail, and nearly sixty of their buildings were partially wrecked.

Booth watched all of this with dismay. Sometimes it was almost more than he could bear. But when the load seemed the heaviest, a friend always came to help. John Bright, a famous member of Parliament, wrote to Mrs. Booth, "The people who mob you would doubtless have mobbed the apostles. Your faith and patience will prevail. The 'craftsmen' who find 'their craft in danger,' 'the high priests and elders of the people,' whose old-fashioned counsels are disregarded by newly-arrived stirrers-up of men, always complain, and then the governors and magistrates, who may 'care for none of these things,' but who always act 'in the interests of the public peace,' think it best to 'straightly charge these men to speak no more' of Christ."

The fact that such a famous man as John Bright would write to encourage them was wonderful indeed. But the best part of it was that the persecutions made their work grow, gave them publicity, and helped change the Army from an English institution to a world-wide institution. Those officers who were thrown into prison didn't mind as long as they knew it was for the sake of Christ.

In one town where an officer had been imprisoned, the people were so angry about it that thirty thousand of them gathered at the time of his release to shake his hand.

Some who fought the Army did so because they claimed that Booth was getting rich out of it. This, of course, was not true. There were people who were angry with him because he would not accept their personal gifts for himself. What he received was put into a common pool and distributed as it should be. But those who hated the Army were willing to believe anything. They made up a poem about him and set it to music. The words went like this:

> Salvation stock is humming every day,
> Utopia nearer coming — so they say!
> Now when Booth has banked his cash,
> And has cooked the Devil's hash,
> He'll wave his blood-red sash, and away!

Booth merely smiled at such things and kept going. He had more important things to do than to get annoyed!

Whenever he was mobbed, he generally tried to keep going and always to keep smiling. Once when he got up to speak at Ipswich, the crowd started to boo him. Taking care that he had a smile and a good attitude, he began to imitate them by returning their boos. His good spirits won over the crowd, and some who came to jeer remained to pray.

Once at the great steel center of Sheffield, a Salvation Army parade was attacked by a bunch of hoodlums who called themselves "The Sheffield Blades." They threw sticks and stones at the leading officers. A local officer, Davidson, was struck on the head with a short club and was nearly killed. Instead of hiding in the carriage in which he rode in order to protect his life, General Booth stood up and urged his troops to salute the people. Many stones whizzed by his head and he was struck several times with mud, but he was not seriously injured. He continued on serenely, as if nothing had happened, to Albert Hall where he helped lead a Council of War.

One of the men who traveled a lot with Booth in those days had been a champion wrestler. There were times when the meetings might have been broken up except for him. Many of the bullies feared him and did nothing; others who interfered were gently tossed out.

Dealing with ruffians was such a common thing that Booth wrote to his officers instructing them that they should never retaliate, but should always smile and show good will.

During these trying times, Kate did what she could to strengthen her husband. He seldom made an important

Booth's beloved "Kate"

One of the Army's "colleges"

decision without first consulting her. Years before, a heck-
ler who felt that Booth was assuming too much power demanded of him, "Are not two heads better than one?"

"It's according to the heads!" snapped Booth, and then
returned to his sermon.

He had great respect for Kate's wisdom, and when
she was sick, which was often, he was very patient and
kind with her. He declared again and again that he could
have done nothing without her help. Although feeble in
body, she was an excellent speaker, and time and time
again she won the day in big public meetings for the Salvation Army. There were few buildings in England that
were too big for her to fill with eager listeners.

When opposition would reach a peak, Mrs. Booth would
urge the officers to "fix bayonets." By this she meant they
should stand firm and do that which they knew to be right
regardless of the consequences. The troops thought of her
as the "Mother" of the Army. She never allowed her illness
to interrupt her husband's work.

A Sunday afternoon service on the lawn of Chicago's School for Officers' Training

Cadets of the Eastern Territory School for Officers' Training participate in a National Salvation Army Week Rally at Rockefeller Plaza in New York City. At podium is Commissioner Holland French, Territorial Commander

Many times she was forced to watch the growth of the Army from her bed, but the growth was so great that she often got up and wrote articles or edited papers in spite of the way she felt. By 1880 there were 876 outposts and nearly ten thousand people who gave their full time to the work. There were thirty colleges where cadets were given six months' training before being allowed to engage the enemy in hand-to-hand combat.

Villages were also evangelized by "Calvary forts." These forts were large vans which were drawn from village to village. Nine officers traveled with each van and hundreds and thousands of people were saved through this method.

Unlike Alexander the Great who wanted to conquer the world for himself, William Booth wanted to conquer the world for Christ. When the time came that all of England was hearing the message, he determined that he would "invade" other countries.

Chapter Seven

Kate's Chariot

As THE YEARS FLED BY, his desire to win souls increased. He talked about the lost day and night. He could think of no other subject, unless it was some scheme to help the poor so that he could lead them to Christ. One night, complaining of a headache, he wrapped a wet towel around his head. And then, thrusting his hands deep into the pockets of his long yellow dressing gown, he proceeded to pace back and forth through the house.

"What are you doing, General?" asked Bramwell, gravely concerned. "You should have been in bed long ago!"

The general glanced quickly at his son. "Bramwell," he muttered fiercely, "I'm thinking! I'm thinking!"

"What are you thinking about, General?"

Booth threw up his hands in a gesture of despair. "Bramwell, I'm thinking of the people's sin! What will the people do with their sin?"

Whenever he was in the presence of an officer, he would cry, "Go for souls and go for the worst!"

At the age of fifty-nine, Kate noticed that a lump had formed in her breast. Her mother had died of cancer and she was worried. Booth sent her to Sir James Paget, one of the finest surgeons in London. After a careful examination, he shook his head, "I'm afraid, Mrs. Booth, that you have cancer," he informed her as gently as he could.

"Are — are you sure?" she asked, her pulse quickening.

70

Catherine Booth was an excellent speaker

"No, I'm not positive. I think maybe you'd better go to someone else and see what they have to say."

Kate went to another doctor, and he confirmed Sir James' diagnosis. "How l-long do you think I can live?" she asked.

"I can't say exactly, but I would estimate that you will have another two years."

"Two years!" exclaimed Kate, thinking of all the work to be done.

"I'm sorry," said the doctor. "We'll do all we can. Maybe a little rest . . . ."

But Kate wasn't listening. She stumbled out to the street and called a cab. On the way home, she sank to the floor on her prayer-worn knees and pled with God to spare her life.

Booth was busy at his desk when she returned with the sad news.

"I'm scheduled to go to Holland," said the general, "but I'll cancel the trip. Someone else can go. I'll stay with you. . . ."

Kate gripped his hand. "William," she said, interrupting him and giving it a tight squeeze, "you promised to go, and you must go. God will take care of me. I'm ready to die. Many of the people over there are not."

He went to Holland and preached, and then hurried back to his wife. Catherine was still able to get around, and since she knew her time on earth was short, she did all she could in the work of the Lord. She wrote letters; she made suggestions to her husband; she spoke before large audiences. But as she did all of these things, there was a spirit of sadness in the house, for everyone knew she was doomed.

She sought a cure through the Mattei treatment, and for a time the treatment stopped some of her pain. But soon it became evident she would have to do something else. Help from the Mattei treatment was only temporary. She decided to try something else. The surgeons persuaded her to submit to an operation.

After the operation, which some think was a mistake, her pain increased. Friends, knowing her love of the sea, arranged for her to be moved to Clanton. And here she lay, propped up in bed, a Bible in her hand.

During this pitiful time Booth was busy writing the most important book of his career, *In Darkest England*. He was writing to help the people to see the grinding poverty that was eating out the heart of their great country. The title, *In Darkest England*, had been chosen because the people were then shuddering over H. M. Stanley's recently published, *In Darkest Africa*.

But writing a book with a dying wife in another room was not an easy thing. There were days when he couldn't set down a single word. If it had not been for the poverty he'd seen, he would have given up.

By looking at a page or two of his diary, we can see some of the horror he was passing through. "My darling," he wrote in his big, difficult way, "had a night of agony. When I went into her room at 2 a.m. she had not closed her eyes. . . . They were endeavoring to staunch a fresh hemorrhage. Everything was saturated with blood."

At another time he scrawled, "She exclaimed again and again as she started with the stabbing pains, 'Oh, these fiery scorpions! these fiery scorpions!'"

The doctors wanted to give her morphine to ease the pain, but she refused. Booth himself pled with her to take it and get some rest. But she still refused. She declared that God was all she needed.

Often the children would find their father marching up and down the hall, his hands over his face, weeping like a child. Sometimes they would hear him cry out in anguish. of spirit, "I don't understand it! I don't understand it!"

People all over the world were interested in her brave struggle with death, and she was interested in them. Whenever she had the strength to do so, she would send messages of encouragement. "Tell the officers," she said to her daughter Emma, "that the only consolation for a Salvationist on his dying bed is to feel he has been a soul winner. Also tell them that after all my labors, I still feel I come far short of the prize of my high calling."

One afternoon as Emma was dressing her wounds she said, "'You need not hurry, Emma, there is plenty of time. I have no train to catch. I have nothing to catch now -- but the chariot!"

She constantly encouraged her husband to finish the book. He would go to his study and work on it for a while, and then he would come rushing back to the bedroom to see how Kate was getting along. She liked music, and sometimes he would kneel by her bed and sing some famous Salvation Army song.

One of the doctors was not a believer and Kate did what she could to win him for Christ. There is no record to indicate that she succeeded, but the world marveled that she made the try — suffering as she did.

The sun was just flaming red in the sky on October 4, 1890 when she was summoned home. The night before had been one of torrential rain. Thunder had shaken the windows. But the day was calm. Larks could be heard, and there was the soft murmur of the surf beating against the nearby shore.

Her remains were placed in a plain oak coffin. A memorial service was conducted in the great Olympia auditorium where tens of thousands came for a last look. The coffin was then taken through the crowded streets of London to Abney Park Cemetery. There was an uninterrupted throng four miles long that stood with heads uncovered as the funeral procession moved on.

Admission to the cemetery had been iimited to ten thousand. And since the crowd wanted to be sure to get in, thousands of them had come as much as two hours early.

The service was conducted by Commissioner Railton.

Booth, though shaken with grief, knew that his beloved Kate had merely gone with the chariot and that it was just a goodnight. With this faith, he stood in front of the grave and gave an eloquent tribute to the frail woman who had held up his hands for forty years. The *Daily Telegraph* reported it well:

> It was a most touching sight when the tall, upright General came forward in the gathering darkness to tell his comrades of the loss he, their chief, had sustained. He spoke manfully, resolutely, and without the slightest trace of affectation. Not a suspicion of clap-trap marred the dignity of the address. He spoke as a soldier should who had disciplined his emotion, without effort and straight from the heart. Few wives who have comforted their husbands for forty years have received such a tribute of honest, glowing praise. It is clear enough where the strength of the Salvation Army is to be found, where its courage, its indomitable energy, where its unswervingness of purpose. To hear General Booth speak, and to see the man, is to understand a great deal of the Salvation Army.

75

A brass plate, bearing the following inscription, was
placed over her grave:

CATHERINE BOOTH
THE MOTHER OF
THE SALVATION ARMY
Born 17th January, 1829
Died 4th October, 1890
"More than conqueror"

It was hard for Booth to face the empty chair at home.
But he kept his mind on others and on other things. He
tried to do the work of a dozen people. He worked on his
book with all his might. The Lord had sent a great editor
to help him. This man, W. T. Stead, had supported the
Army for years. He refused to join, but he lent a strong
and able hand from the outside. He took Booth's work and
arranged it as it should be arranged and made necessary
corrections.

Then one evening the work was done. He leafed
through the big pile of manuscript and prayed that God
would use it to stir, not only England, but the whole world.
Friends who had read portions of it thought it was a little
strong. But Booth knew the poverty of England well. His
words were strong because of what he had seen. Dante
dipped his pen in the dark pool of his imagination to write
his terrible Inferno. Booth didn't have the imagination of
Dante, but he didn't need it. He just put down what he
had seen. He described the slums; the plight of the family
man without work; the dilemma of the released convict
seeking employment.

But the purpose of the book was not just to describe
the pit; it was also to suggest a way out. He proposed having factories for the destitute where they could earn enough

76

for their food and lodging. He described at length an employment agency that could be set up to help men find work. He outlined a force of collectors to be known as a "Household Salvage Brigade" to go through the streets and gather discarded clothes and other items that could be used by families in need. He suggested overseas colonies where the discouraged and destitute could be sent to start a new life.

In order to get these things going, he decided they would have to have one hundred thousand pounds.

Satisfied that the work was the best he could do, he added a sheet to the front and wrote a beautiful dedication to Kate and then sent the book to the printers.

The moment the book came from the press, things started humming. Professor Huxley, an old enemy of the Army, considered Booth a fanatic and published scathing articles against the scheme in *The Times*. But there were

The headstone on William and Catherine's grave

many others who thought enough of it to give large contributions.

The morning after the book was published, Booth was ascending the stairs at his headquarters when he was stopped by a man whom he had never seen before.

"General Booth, I believe," he said, extending his hand.

"Yes, sir," replied the General.

"I have been reading the critique in *The Times* of your 'Darkest England Scheme.' I believe your plan is good, and I want to give you the first thousand pounds."

Another man, a prominent member of the Stock Exchange, called at his office. "I want to ask you a question — only one. I want to know whether you are going to give religion alongside your other benefits to these people whom you seek to help? I am not a religious man myself. I am not saved and never shall be — I am a lost soul; but there is no reason why these poor wretches should not have religion; and if you will give them religion, I will help you."

When Booth assured him the Gospel would be preached, he handed him five hundred pounds in cash.

The book sold much more rapidly than Booth had ever dreamed. It earned twenty thousand pounds and the General turned all of the money over to the Scheme. In a very short time, one hundred and four thousand pounds had been collected.

The Scheme was tried, and it proved to be only partially successful. Overseas colonies were founded, but they didn't manage to accomplish all that Booth had hoped. One reason for this was that the people who gave so generously in the beginning did not keep it up. Another reason was that many of the officers lacked experience in this kind of thing. Nevertheless, thousands of souls were saved and the attention of the world was focused on the Salvation Army as it never had been before.

78

Chapter Eight

The Invasion of America

WHEN THE DAY CAME FOR BOOTH to sail for his first invasion of America, there were many officers who went down to see the ship off. As it was disappearing into the distance one of the commissioners heard a bystander remark, "So he's off?"

"Yes, he's gone," replied the officer sadly.

"And when do you go?" asked the man.

"Go? What do you mean?"

"Well, you will never see him again now, will you?"

At that moment the commissioner began laughing, for he remembered how the enemies of the Army had declared that after Booth had banked a lot of cash, he would sail away with it. This story became a joke in the Army, and the officers have been laughing about it ever since.

Actually, when Booth left for America there were already more than five hundred officers over here. Many of these were Americans. The first corps had been raised up by a family that had moved from England to Philadelphia.

On his first tour of the United States, he was greeted with enthusiasm, and this enthusiasm increased with each visit. In 1902 he had such a wonderful welcome he described it at length to a friend, and we will quote part of his letter here.

"Well, I have been busy and no mistake. Day after day, hour after hour, you might say minute after minute, I have had duties calling for immediate attention. Oh, it

General William Booth

has been a whirl! But what a wonderful rush of success the nine weeks have been since I landed at New York.

"The people, the press, the dignitaries of all classes have combined in the heartiest welcomes ever given in this country, I suppose, to a 'foreigner' of any nationality. It has been remarkable, and, indeed, surprising, for it was so largely unexpected.

"I have just come into this city of Kansas. The two largest hotels have competed to have the privilege of giving me their best rooms, with free entertainment. A monster brewery that illumines the whole city every night with a searchlight has been running alternate slides, one saying, 'Buy our lager beer,' and the other 'General Booth at the Convention Hall Monday night.' The building for my meeting tonight will hold 8,000 people, and on Saturday 4,000 tickets were already sold."

When he landed in New York, seventy-three bombs were set off, each one indicating a year of his life already lived. Philadelphia greeted him with parades and gave him the key to the city. At Washington he was received by the President and prayed before the Senate. The Senate chamber that morning was unusually crowded and the galleries were packed out because the news had gotten around that he would lead in prayer. He had been told that his prayer should not be longer than three minutes, and above all, it should not exceed six minutes! But as he stood there, his flowing white beard on his chest, he could only think of God's goodness to him and the Salvation Army. We are told that he didn't stop at the three minute period, but that he did manage to say "amen" before six minutes were up!

After the "amen," a motion was passed that the prayer be recorded in the Records of the House.

Colonel Lawley, who often sang solos and led the sing-

Booth addresses a crowd during one of his motorcade campaigns

ing in his meetings, traveled with him throughout America.
He taught tens of thousands to sing:

Oh, the drunkard may come,
Or the swearer may come;
Backsliders and sinners are all welcome home.
If you will but believe
And be washed in the blood,
For ever and ever you will dwell with the Lord.

John Lawley had great success in getting people to
go forward. At one of the great meetings in Exeter Hall,
Lawley stepped forward to the rail around the pulpit at
the conclusion of Booth's sermon and said, "Who will lead
the way to Jesus? Who will start the procession to Calvary's
fountain?"

"I will," shouted a twelve-year-old boy. Two hundred
and forty-two men and women followed him.

At San Francisco, Booth was asked to speak to a group
of Chinese in Chinatown. Realizing that he had a great
opportunity, he preached to his Oriental audience with all
his heart. When he gave the invitation, many crowded forward to accept Christ. But sitting on a front seat was a
huge Chinese who refused to move. He had been deeply
stirred by the message and his large dark eyes were damp
with tears, but he would not budge.

Finally an officer went to him and asked him to go
forward.

The Chinaman shook his head sadly and sobbed, "Jesus
Him blave man — me no blave man."

"But look at Colonel Lawley; he came," pled the officer,
pointing to the singer on the platform.

The man replied, "Yes, he velly blave man — me no
blave man."

"But look at the general — he came."

83

"Yes, the genel, he blave man too. Me no blave man."

Booth heard this part of the conversation, went down, and extending his hand invited, "Come, my brother, you be brave, too. Come!"

The man responded immediately. He knelt at the altar while an officer explained the way of salvation from the Word. He prayed in Chinese for a moment, and then he leaped to his feet and with a wonderful look of happiness on his face exclaimed, "Now me heap blave man!"

William H. Nelson, in his fine book, *Blood and Fire,* tells of Booth's visit to St. Louis:

"The largest auditorium in the city was secured, and it was packed to capacity. He spoke for an hour, giving a very interesting story of his life. He told of his birth, his struggles as a boy, his preaching on the streets of London, his seven years as a Methodist preacher and evangelist. He then told of going to Whitechapel when every one else had

Colonel Lawley traveled with Booth throughout America

neglected that place, and starting, without any human aid, his work to rescue the lost. From one man standing in the midst of that spiritual wilderness, the work had grown until it now covered the whole world. He told of the countries in which the Army was laboring, gave the number of officers and soldiers, and gave an interesting description of the social work. The vast audience was interested, but nothing special had been done for them. The meeting lacked that spiritual glow which usually attended his meetings.

"But suddenly he drew himself up to his full height, and, throwing out in a dramatic way his right hand, he pointed his index finger. It seemed to many as if he were pointing directly at them. He looked like an Old Testament prophet standing there with his tall, majestic form, his flowing hair, and his long white beard. And a prophet he was, for he could call men to righteousness and he could speak the words which would lead to a resurrection and a life for backslidden and lukewarm souls.

"The dramatic intensity which suddenly electrified that audience reminded them in a startling way of the prophet Amos standing before the listless and materialistic nation where every man was going his own way, with none deeply concerned for the work of God. They were concerned for their own welfare, but not for the house of God and the kingdom of God. The whole atmosphere of the meeting changed in a second. The air was electric. Men and women gripped themselves tensely. There was a deathlike stillness; and then in a voice quivering with emotion and spiritual intensity, Booth thundered out, 'That's what I've done with my life; what are you going to do with yours?'" *

He went from one triumph to another, but the one that

* From *Blood and Fire* by William H. Nelson. Copyright, 1929, Century Company. Used by special permission.

pleased him the most, outside of souls being saved, was the change of attitude in America toward the Army. In the beginning many Americans resented the fact that the Army was directed from England.

To his friend John Cory, who had supported him for years, he wrote, "I had reason to believe that a great change had taken place in public feeling toward the Army and towards the General in particular . . . but I was not prepared for the welcome which met me. It was not merely the crowds who came to the meeting in spite of the most unfavorable weather . . . but it was the friendliness of the Press. . . . No buildings that we have been able to secure, have been large enough for the Sunday and evening attendances. In some places the fights outside for admission have been really dangerous, limbs have been fractured. . . .

"I have been here nine weeks, during which time I have conducted ninety-three heavy meetings, travelled some 7,500 miles, seen 1,150 souls at the penitent-form, written articles for the Press, done a large amount of correspondence, transacted a great deal of business, and held almost constant communion with my people.... ."

On his return to England he was received with pride. Dinners were given in his honor, and the newspapers, as a whole, praised his success: But he didn't have time to be lionized. More citadels had to be established, more forts of the enemy had to be stormed and taken.

He established homes for girls who had gotten into trouble; he planned an organization to help former convicts get employment; he invaded Australia and soon had hundreds of officers at work. At this time his mail frequently amounted to five thousand letters a year. Nevertheless he still had time for those who needed help. Whenever he had the chance he preached to prisoners. He felt that they were no worse than many on the outside and that God wanted to save them.

A friend of his tells how on a certain Monday afternoon he stood in front of 700 long-term prisoners to preach the Gospel. This was in the year 1910 and prisoners were not treated as well then as they are now. They sat silently as he preached, for they were strictly forbidden to make a sound. At the close of his sermon Booth declared, "The chaplain will help you, the authorities will help you, the wardens will help you."

This, in spite of the rule to be quiet, brought a shout of bitter laughter from the convicts. Somewhat embarrassed, Booth added, "The Salvation Army will help you!"

The memory of the incident stirred the General's righteous indignation, and he determined to do something about it. He decided that England would have to investigate its prisons and improve them.

Going from office to office with his grievance, he finally found himself in the plush office of Mr. Winston Churchill, then Home Secretary of the United Kingdom.

They discussed several aspects of the problem and Churchill promised to do what he could to help the situation. As Booth stood to go, the future prime minister and Nobel Prize winning author held out his hand, and with a smile enquired, "Well, General, am I converted now?"

This question was rather point blank, but it demanded an answer. Booth wanted to please him, so that he would use his influence for prison reform; at the same time he had to be true to the Word that he had been witnessing to him, and so he replied, "Oh, no! I wouldn't say you're converted, but I think you're convicted!"

Churchill admired Booth for his courage and once declared, "The three most famous generals I have known in my life won no battles over foreign foe, yet their names, which all begin with B, are household words.

"They are General Baden-Powell, the Boy Scouts' Association; General Botha, United South Africa; and General Booth of the Salvation Army."

Chapter Nine

World Fame

HE HAD NEVER SOUGHT FAME — his only desire was to serve the Master. But fame came to him and increased each year. In 1905, at a great meeting presided over by the Lord Mayor, he was given the freedom of the city of London. When he was asked to speak, he gave all the credit for his work to the Lord. We will quote just one paragraph of his speech here. "My life has been a continual fight. Ever since, some sixty years ago, I turned my back upon a world of ease and show, and entered on this battlefield to fight for the honor of my heavenly King and for the salvation of the lost, there has seldom been a day in which some bewildering perplexity has not come to my mind. . . . But still the arms of Jehovah have sustained me. . . ."

Two years later he received a letter from Lord Curzon, asking him to come to Oxford University to receive an honorary Doctor of Civil Law degree. The letter promised that he would not have to make a speech and that he could rent the necessary cap and gown. Apparently Curzon knew he would resent spending money for something as useless as a cap and gown when such money could buy food for the poor!

As old age crept up on him, he found it necessary to get someone to be with him at all times. Many of the officers, knowing that such a position was open, longed for the job — for traveling throughout the world with the Gen-

Booth received an honorary Doctor of Civil Laws degree from Oxford University in 1907

eral was indeed a great opportunity. The man finally chosen was J. Evan Smith, and fortunately for us, he wrote a book about some of his experiences entitled *Booth the Beloved.*

It was this man's duty to arrange for rooms and railway tickets and so on. He soon learned the General hated to waste time. If he happened to get him to the station five minutes before the train was to leave, he would scold, "Now you're happy — having got me here too soon. What will these people think of me wasting time like this? They'll think I have nothing else to do."

If he had to change trains and there was an hour or two of delay, he always wanted a meeting arranged so he could preach and win a few more souls. He wanted to use every opportunity for the Lord.

Once when he was preaching in Berlin, there were some caged lions near the building in which he spoke. As the general began to wax eloquent, the lions started to roar. Immediately he used the incident to advantage by telling his audience of "the devil, as a roaring lion, walking about seeking whom he may devour."

He was very particular about what he ate and drank. He never touched meat of any kind. His favorite drink was hot tea, diluted with a good supply of boiled milk. If he happened to be a guest in some home where the tea was lukewarm, he would motion for the maid to come and then he would whisper, "I like my tea as I like my religion — hot, very hot." And all of the maids, as far as he was concerned, were named Mary!

He liked to pray wherever he was. Sometimes he would say, "Fetch the girls and we'll have a final word of prayer." The servants would then gather, and he would lead in prayer. There were times when the host and servants were embarrassed, but he never was.

91

Booth loved his Bible

This habit of prayer was taught to his children, and the lesson was well learned. Years later, after his death and after Bramwell had become the general, Bramwell was on a ship going to Auckland. There had been a dreadful storm. Some of the passengers were certain they would never make port. In a tense moment of panic, Bramwell engaged the captain in conversation. When they were ready to part, he said, "Captain, I know you are trying to bring us into the harbor at Auckland safe and well, but I wonder if you are making for the heavenly harbor?" He then asked the skipper to bow his head while he led in prayer.

When they opened their eyes, the captain shook Bramwell's hand and said, "Thank you, General Booth. Do you know you are the only man who has prayed with me since your dear old father crossed over on this same ship fifteen years ago!"

During a time of great tension between South Africa and England, General Booth found himself in a train bound for London with the famous Cecil Rhodes. As they were riding along, Booth touched Rhodes' arm. "I want to speak to you about yourself," he said, peering at him with his dark eyes. "You're a man with much depending on you just now. Tell me, how is it with your soul?"

This man, who had probably done more than anyone else to carve out the African section of the British Empire, replied, "Well, General, it's not quite so well with my soul as I could wish."

"Do you pray?" continued Booth.

"Sometimes; not quite so often as I should."

"Will you let me pray with you — now?"

They knelt on the floor of the carriage and Booth prayed that God would bless him and save his soul. When they got up, Rhodes pressed the general's hand and said, "I hope you will continue to pray for me."

J. Evan Smith has recorded for us one of his typical prayers. Smith had helped him into bed and was in the act of leaving when the general motioned him back to pray. "O Lord," he prayed, "we do thank Thee for the hope Thou hast given me today of recovery, in order to do a little more work for Thee and for the dying souls around. Bless Smith here; help him to help me — help him in his soul — let the fire burn in his heart, that he may not only help me with his typing, but help me by the fire of his soul. O God, do bless the chief, the commander, and American affairs, and the Army all over the world. For Jesus Christ's sake, our Saviour. Amen."

A ship on which he was traveling stopped at a New Zealand port, and since he was the most famous man on board, a large group of famous newsmen approached him for an interview. Booth gladly consented. He answered all their questions. He posed for pictures. He told them stories. When they were through he said, "Have I answered all your questions?"

The men nodded that he had.

"Well then, having given you a half hour of my time, I'm now going to ask you for some of yours," announced the general, his eyes flashing. In a moment he was on his knees asking that God would bless the journalists and help them to be a blessing to all of New Zealand.

Booth never concluded an interview of any kind without putting in some message about the Lord, and many men — some famous, some unknown — were won this way.

In his book, *Something for Myself*, Rudyard Kipling tells of his meeting with the general on board ship. ". . . I saw him walking backward in the dusk over the uneven

wharf, his cloak blown upwards, tulip-fashion, over his grey
head, while he beat a tambourine in the face of the singing,
weeping, praying crowd who had come to see him off. . . .

"I saw no more of him until I had picked up my P.&O.
. . . Here all the world came out in paddle boats and small
craft to speed him on his road to India. . . . I talked much
with General Booth during that voyage. Like the young
ass I was, I expressed my distaste at his appearance on In-
vercargill wharf. 'Young feller,' he replied, bending great
brows at me, 'if I thought I could win *one* more soul to
the Lord by walking on my head and playing the tambourine with my toes, I'd — I'd learn how.'

"He had the right of it ('if by any means I can save
some') and I had the decency to apologize.

". . . The next time I met him was at Oxford when de-
grees were being conferred. He strode across to me in his
Doctor's robes, which magnificently became him, and, 'Young
feller,' said he, 'how's your soul?' "

He was received by royalty in many of the countries
of Europe and around the world. But never did he take
any of these occasions for self-glory. He was glad he had
them and reported them to the press, but he was simply
glad because they furthered the work of the Army and of
winning souls.

Many people tried to get him to accept personal gifts,
but he generally managed to refuse. Having heard him say
that he had not had a vacation in twenty years, a wealthy
lady wrote, "General, if you will only take a holiday, I'll
place at your disposal my house and my horses and carriage;
and, in addition, I'll give you five thousand pounds for that
new scheme of yours."

Booth told the story to his secretary and then he

growled, "Smith, I'm not taking any holiday, but I'm after that five thousand pounds." And, what's more, we are told that he got the five thousand pounds without having to take a vacation, and a lot more money besides!

As he moved from city to city, he continued to work on his books and at his vast correspondence. His secretary would place the typewriter on the seat of a railway carriage and then kneel on the floor to type while Booth dictated. At night a wire was stretched between the two men, and if Booth couldn't sleep he would ring for Smith. Many a letter was answered in the middle of the night while the founder bumped over a railway between one town and another. He was determined that every minute would count.

Speaking night after night and sleeping in different beds each time is extremely hard work. It has completely worn out many a young man. But Booth did not let such hardships bother him. He continued to travel right up until he was taken home. Sometimes, however, he got a little weary. When he was eighty years of age, he jotted down in his diary, "I wonder how many different homes I have been in and in how many different beds I have slept. I am very tired, but I must go on — on — on. I cannot stand still. . . . A fire is in my bones! . . . Souls, souls, souls, my heart hungers for souls!"

But as zealous as he was, he was gradually running down. To a group of Philadelphia reporters he said, "I haven't had a day off in fourteen years, but I'll die pretty soon, and the first thing I'll ask for in heaven is a six months' vacation."

His eyesight was growing dim and he found it more and more difficult to eat what people cooked for him. This last problem finally became so acute that his secretary prepared a menu and had copies sent on ahead. From it we can see that his diet was very simple.

"Dear Friend," began the letter, "I am informed that you have very kindly undertaken to entertain General Booth during his visit to your town, and, as his requirements are somewhat unusual — though very simple — feel sure you will welcome the information as to his needs which we have the pleasure to give below.

"The General does not take fish, flesh, or fowl in any shape or form.

"The following will be all he desires:

"Tea, about 4:30: Strong Ceylon tea, boiling hot milk, white bread, dry toast and butter, with the addition of a few fried potatoes (or mushrooms, if convenient)."

He frequently teased a doctor friend by asking why he didn't diet his patients. Then he would answer the question himself by declaring that if the doctor did this, they would all get well and he would have no more patients!

On his last trip in America his daughter Eva persuaded him to lie down on the sofa and made him promise that he wouldn't get up until she brought him a cup of tea. But she had only been gone a few minutes when she returned to find him pacing back and forth, his wrinkled cheeks wet with tears.

"Darling!" she admonished, "you promised me you wouldn't move."

"Oh, I know, I know!" he replied with a wave of his hand, "but I've been thinking of all the sufferings of little children, the children of the great cities, and I can't rest, I can't rest."

He returned to England in 1912 to do some administrative work. From Smith's diary, we learn of an accident he had at this time that proved to be the beginning of the end. "After the General had rested in the afternoon, on descending the first flight of stairs from his room, he missed the last step and fell full length, striking his head; but he was not hurt, and gathering himself up, exclaimed, 'I always told you my head was the hardest part of me.'"

His trouble was that he was getting so that he could not see, but he said as little about it as possible, for he didn't want to worry his friends.

Chapter Ten

Promotion to Glory

AN OPERATION ON HIS EYES was not a success, and he lost one eye completely. But feeling that another operation might restore the other eye, he agreed to submit to it if the surgeons would perform it in his home.

Before his operations he preached to ten thousand people in London's Albert Hall. He concluded his address by saying with a chuckle, "I am going into dry dock for repairs." He was certain he would again have clear vision.

On May 23, the day scheduled for the second operation, he was unusually cheerful. He went to his study, dictated several short letters and signed some documents that awaited his signature. Then his picture was taken with Colonel Kitching and his faithful sheep dog, Gyp.

The operation was performed in the afternoon at three o'clock. The doctors remarked that he was an ideal patient. They felt that the operation was a success and that he would see again, provided there was no infection.

Two days later, however, it was found that infection had set in and that the old warrior would never see again. The surgeons hated to tell him what had happened, so they asked Bramwell to break the news.

Bramwell entered the dark room, and taking his father's hand in his own, said gently, "I'm afraid, I-I'm afraid that you w-will never see again."

"You mean that I'm blind?" exclaimed Booth.

"Well, General, I-I think so."

Evangeline kneels beside her father's chair

"Does this mean I-I'll never see your face again?"
"No, not in this world."

There was a long pause, and then General Booth said in a voice that was remarkably calm, "God must know best!"

After another pause the old man squeezed his son's hand while he said, "Bramwell, I have done what I could for God and for the people with my eyes. Now I shall do what I can for God and for the people without my eyes."

Confined now to bed, he continued to do as much for the Lord as possible by dictating letters and encouraging those who gathered around him. He never thought of himself; it was always *others*.

One morning while a strike was raging in East London, a servant brought him an egg for breakfast. He pushed the tray away muttering, "How can I eat eggs when women and children are starving! Poor women can't get milk to feed their babes and you bring me an egg!"

Two months later he was able to get up and sit in an armchair. He felt that the time had come to get those about him to make some serious promises. One afternoon he asked for Bramwell to come and sit close. Then he said, "Bramwell, I want you to promise that when my voice is silent and I am gone from you, you will use what influence you may possess with the Army to do more for the homeless of the world, the homeless men. Mind! I am not thinking of this country only, but of all lands. Also take care of the homeless women, and the homeless children. Oh, the children! Bramwell, look after the homeless."

After Bramwell had promised to do this, the old man continued, "I have been thinking very much during the last few nights of China. I greatly regret that the Lord has not

101

*General William Booth's funeral cortege passing through
the heart of London*

permitted me to raise our flag amongst that wonderful people. I want you to promise me that as soon as possible you will get together a party of suitable officers and unfurl our flag in that wonderful land. . . . You will need money. I know that; but you will get the money if you get the right people."

"You promise?" he asked, after a lengthy pause.

"I promise," said Bramwell.

"Then give me your hand on it," replied the general.

They clasped hands and then prayed together. When Bramwell opened his eyes, a stream of light flooded the room, and played on his father's snowy white head. Bramwell never forgot this scene.

One evening after an unusually restless day his secretary asked if there wasn't something he could do for him to revive his spirits. "Yes, Smith," he stammered, "take me — take me . . . to a meeting . . . and let me hear . . . dear old Lawley say . . . 'General . . . here . . . comes . . . the fortieth soul.' "

As the days went by he sank lower and lower. But sometimes he would feel a little better. On one of these occasions, he remarked to Bramwell, "I'm leaving you a bonnie handful!" Bramwell, of course, knew that his father had chosen him as the new general.

In the afternoon on the twentieth of August, there was a violent thunderstorm. The storm passed and the evening was quiet. That night, at thirteen minutes past ten, the old warrior, victor of a thousand campaigns, breathed his last.

His last coherent words were spoken under great difficulties, but those who heard them treasured them in their hearts. He had been sitting in his chair talking of some

103

*Bramwell Booth gives final address before his father's coffin
is lowered at Abney Park, London*

incident of the day. Then he suddenly exclaimed, "Bram-well — the promises . . ." But he was unable to go on. "The promises . . ." he tried again. But again he could not complete the sentence. Determined to express what was on his mind he tried a third time, "The promises . . ." This time when he faltered, someone supplied the missing words, "of God." He tried a fourth time, and with much difficulty was successful, "The promises — of — God — are sure — are sure — if you will only believe."

Headlined in the newspapers the next day was the statement: "THE GENERAL HAS LAID DOWN HIS SWORD."

Telegrams from all over the world poured into the Salvation Army headquarters. Hundreds of newspapers carried the story and each paper tried to outdo the other in praise.

His body lay in state in a plain coffin made of pine in Congress Hall. Sixty-five thousand people marched by to take a last look at the man who hated poverty as much as he loved Christ. His soldiers would have liked to have used an elaborate casket, but Booth had left instructions that money was not to be wasted in such a way.

Forty bands assembled for the last services and they played the battle songs he had loved so well.

On Thursday afternoon his body was carried to its last resting place in Abney Park Cemetery. The streets of London were lined with tens of thousands, and as the body of the old soldier of the cross was carried down the thoroughfare, handkerchiefs everywhere touched overflowing eyes.

Ten thousand Salvationists marched behind. There were hundreds of flags. Traffic in the great city was held up for hours. But in the whole proceedings, there was a note of triumph, for everyone knew that General Booth had been promoted to glory.

A simple shield was placed over his grave bearing the following inscription:

WILLIAM BOOTH

FOUNDER AND 1ST GENERAL OF

THE SALVATION ARMY

Born 1829

Born again of the Spirit 1845

Founded the Salvation Army 1865

Went to heaven 20th August 1912

BIBLIOGRAPHY

Blood and Fire, by William H. Nelson (The Century Co., 1929).

I Was a Stranger, by Harold C. Steele (Exposition Press, 1954).

Something of Myself, by Rudyard Kipling (Doubleday Doran, 1937).

The War Romance of the Salvation Army, by Evangeline Booth and Grace Livingtone Hill (J. B. Lippincott, 1919).

The Life of General William Booth, 2 Volumes, by Harold Begbie (Macmillan, 1920).

Booth the Beloved, by J. Evan Smith (Oxford University Press, 1949).

The Authoritative Life of General Booth, by George S. Railton (Salvationist Publishing and Supplies, Ltd., 1912).

I Was There, by F. Hayter Cox (Salvationist Publishing and Supplies, Ltd.).

Memoirs of Catherine Booth, 2 Volumes, by F. de L. Booth-Tucker (Fleming H. Revell, 1892).

The Army Today

Former Vice President Richard M. Nixon chats with Major and Mrs. Jack Cheyne, managers of an Evangeline Residence for young business women. There are 16 such residences in the U. S.

A Salvation Army Emergency Canteen serves police, government inspectors and others at the scene of the Electra jet crack-up near O'Hare Field in Chicago, 1961

*The new Central Territorial Headquarters Building at
860 North Dearborn Street, Chicago 10, Illinois*

Counseling and helpful understanding are just a part of the Army's prison counseling ministry

Cadets training to be officers take part in a street service

Cadets, man and wife, receive commissions as officers during commissioning (ordination) ceremonies in Chicago

Open air meeting conducted by soldiers and converts of the Chicago Harbor Light Center. Major Roland Quinn, commanding officer, is third from right

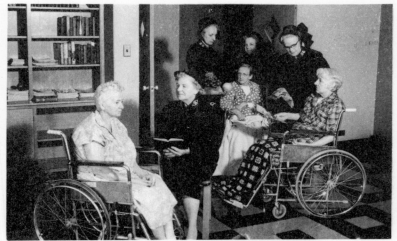

League of Mercy members visit in hospitals

Major Quinn counseling with two members of the Golden Age Club at Harbor Light Center on Chicago's Skid Row

Part of the program at the Detroit Eventide Home is the Department of Arts and Crafts. This is just one of the homes for the aged operated by the Salvation Army

Repairing old furniture makes a new man. These men eventually graduate to employment in normal channels of industry

*At a music camp in Iowa a class of young cornetists
receive instructions*

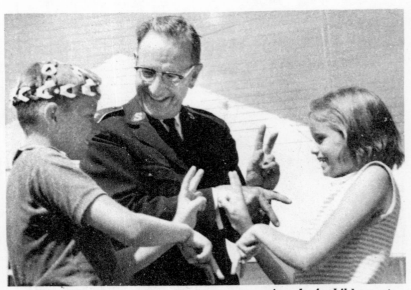

*The Salvation Army operates a camp for deaf children at
Silver Lake, near Minneapolis. More than 100 youngsters
from all parts of Minnesota take part in this camp, originated
by Lt. Col. Thomas V. Gates, center*

A Sunday school class

*A nature study class examines a snake at a Salvation Army
summer camp*

Returning from a flag lowering at a Music Camp conducted for Salvation Army youth, Camp Wonderland, Camp Lake, Wisconsin. The Army operates 54 such camps in the United States

Vivienne Farmer, a Salvation Army "Sunbeam," receives the two highest honors to be given a child by the Minneapolis Fire Department, the Award of Merit and the Junior Fire Marshal badge, for helping to save the lives of four children trapped in a burning duplex

A mass meeting for the funeral service of Commissioner Lawley, conducted by General Bramwell Booth, at rostrum. 5,000 persons attended